NESTS IN AIR

NESTS
IN AIR

POEMS

NATHAN HOKS

Black Ocean
Boston · Detroit · Chicago

Black Ocean
P.O. Box 52030
Boston, MA 02205
blackocean.org

Cover Art and Design by Julian Montague | montagueprojects.com
Book Design by adam b. bohannon | adambohannon.com

ISBN: 978-1-939568-38-0

Library of Congress Control Number: 2021931839

Library of Congress Cataloging-in-Publication Data

FIRST EDITION

Printed in Canada

for Mariana

CONTENTS

❀

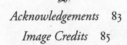

Tranquil bird that flies in reverse bird
That nests in air
At the limit where our soil is already shining
Lower your second eyelid the earth dazzles you
When you raise your head

GUILLAUME APOLLINAIRE

Nests in Air

The light gray bird flies across the fence.
It flummoxes the squirrel and cordons off the yard.
It flies into the office and enters the sentence
I was writing about a bird that lacks ambition
But understands the glimmer of the safety pins
Because its eyes are made of needles.
The bird upchucks a fetus because like all birds
Its body is pain's whistling vehicle.
It shimmers on the bookshelf, whistles a fight song
And pecks at the family portraits
Before building a nest with their radioactive scraps.

What is it thinking? What does it want?
Can it hatch offspring in this fucked up sludge fest?
What is the bird's mood? Is it an apricot?
Masculine? Feminine? Feminine-masculine?
Militant? Militant fruit? Fiery fruit? Bursting flesh?
A fire opening in the sun? A sun burning a crèche?
Where can it leave its brood? In sludge? Rotten fruit?
In radioactive scraps?

When the bird
Flies back to the window, the window becomes its song
And its nest and its throat of blood.

It launches a neighborhood protection program
And from the rosebush assembles the self as a man of thorns,
A big cop whose head is congested
So he pistol-whips himself until the enhanced interrogation
Launches his brains into the sky
Where the bloody pieces become a droning swarm
Blocking out the moonlight, bloodying the sunlight,
Drowning the birdsongs, clogging the throats,
Clustering around the gray bird and ushering its clusters
To the wiry nest, the cradle that hums, the scraps of air.

Stopped in Air

I gulp for air but I have swallowed a stop sign
So my chest cavity expands my rib cage swells
There is a stop sign in my lungs and its essence
Enters my blood my veins my tongue my ears redden
My heart throbs with dark red inhibition
And when I exhale the stop sign spreads white-tipped wings
Into the air it is more potent than any contagion
I'll be quarantined in a glass box where I'll have to wear
A plastic stop sign warped over my face and
The new polyethylene compounds will plug up my nose
And I'll be tortured with a flaming stop sign
They'll hold it over my mouth until my gums vibrate and my teeth melt
They'll tape my eyes shut so I can only see one
Indivisible stop sign hovering over the planet
With liberty and justice for all and they'll lob stop signs
Down on any detractors I can hear them booming
As I type a text message and it is a stop sign
And I pick up my son and he is a stop sign
And I call my parents and they tell me the yard is
A bright green swamp of octagons Dad can't go to work
Because a stop sign spewed red acid on all the machines
I pack up to leave the city but the drawbridge is clogged
With the bloody air of stop signs
A feather takes flight from beneath my boot
Even the dead bird was a stop sign

The Cradle

When I put my baby in the bath
  The water stings his skin.
Something shrill in the eye sings out.

  The dark area of a father waters
The soft area ripping through my glassy
  Eyes. They scan the window

And cannot make out a hill
  Against the imperial purple sky
Since the lantern obliterates self-reflection

  And pushes the subtle winds
Into a deeper unmined past where
  The shrill student I was sketches

His outline in the examination booklet.
  Actually, he never sleeps. He's
A spy camera ripping through the ice-gray flower.

  He drinks from a puddle
Then flits about like some muddy bird

Frantically building a nest
Against the impish purple sky.
   His skin's his cage and fiery

Cradle. Sneezing radiators sprout
   The larval poet's rich embryo,
A spider thrashing in the lake.

Nests in Air

The nest is a warp of conflict. Its twisted reeds
And muddy floor absorb the young squabbles.
Putrid eggs get stuffed behind family photos
And microorganisms chew at the padded walls
While assassinating shadows inch toward the window.

*

They have come to build a new house in my brain.
They have come to slash the hose and destroy the garden.
They have come to scribble with red crayon on the walls
And collect the half-colored coloring books
And turn the spongy pages into a pulpy mush.

*

In the warped nest the robotic sparrow
Peck-peck-pecks at the mush-mush-mush which tastes of old paper
And earth and blue crayon mixed with green crayon
Mixed with chlorine dioxide and maybe some guar gum.
I taste no banana. No omega-3s. My springy jaw
Chomp-chomp-chomps and I fold up in the bedroom where

*

I write a hundred poems in the shapes of birds.
They ask questions about dust bunnies and vaccinations.
They smash their beaks on parenting books.
They launch themselves from windowsills and electric lines.
They spiral-dive to chase each other's unhitched feathers
And their shrill cries awaken the neighborhood patrol.

*

The nest whorls around us. The shadows slip away
And the bird-poems spit pulpy mush all over the cradle
So I paint the window blue and call it the Ocean.
Life-vested children wave sticks in the air. The blue-green
Body swells. When I cough, the whirlpool listens.

Blocking out the moonlight

The polyethylene compounds plug up my nose

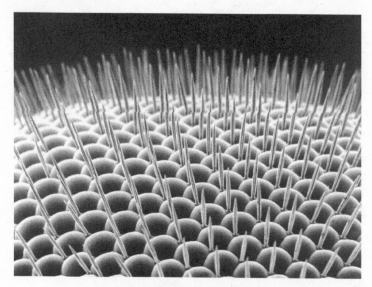

Something shrill in the eye sings out

I peck-peck-peck at the mush-mush-mush

Toy Cloud

The rabbit has stolen
The big bear's pointy red hat

The frog looks longingly
At its evaporating pond

A powerful glow comes
Off the sunflower

So everyone wears goggles
My son rolls around in the ferns

It seems he has overdosed
On sugar cookies

Does he care about the bear's hat?
To him I am a ghost on a bicycle

I remember my father's mouth
Reading aloud beneath his beard

He is hiding in my face
The toy cloud is filled with rain

The Burning Nest

Snoozing in his chair
My dad hears roaring jets
And droning choppers

When I crinkle the newspaper
He sees dazzling gold flecks
Leap from the rainforest

He wakes with a start
He is just like the rest of us
A nest is burning in the tree

The Astronavigator's Nest

It is late so I string a starling to the ceiling.
Its feathers must stay intact and its song
Must brighten the night sky
To guide the solitary travelers to inns
And rest areas, to rivers and streams,

To the new roads we've wondered about,
Dreamed of touching with our feet—
I even see my worn sneakers jostling
The untouched pebbles as dust rises
Toward my rolled cuffs, but the infant nebula

Tells me to clear my throat and remain
A silent spectator lodged in the hang glider's
Windless nightmare, a modality evaporating
Until the particles disengage from the body
And still puddles retain the light.

The Nomads' Nest

The nomads arrive on camels.
They speak in whimpers and their
Cigarette smoke clogs the weather balloons.
Their encampment makes the shape
Of a whispering mouth on the top of the ridge
Where they catch solar rays
And convert them into the sound
Of an excavator scraping its teeth
Across an enormous chalkboard.
But their teeth are floodlights,
The beams warp around the pines,
And their eyes are lake water
Eroding the shoreline.
Their camels smell like camels
And are so soft-hearted they never moan,
Never kick, never glance over their smooth
Muzzles which jut past the camp's atmosphere
Like piers leading the children into
The oxbow lake where they will swim
For an hour before returning for a nap.

A powerful glow

When I crinkle the newspaper

Dust rises toward my rolled cuffs

Beams warp around the pines

A Paper Father's Nest

What if I were a father and all my children were vomiting paper?
Would I write a poem on their paper?

Or would I take them in for an x-ray? And would the doctor suspect
me of negligence? Would they call Child Services? Would I need
to kill the doctor to save my children? Would I have to torch the
hospital and kidnap the nurses?

What if the children liked their vomit-paper? What if they tried to
live with it, kept it in plastic boxes under the bed, colored it, and cut
circles and squares out of it?

What if I were the father of a million particles of paper? What if I
inseminated a paper mill and the whole valley were flooded in papery
pulp? What if I drank the pulp? What if it stimulated my melatonin?
What if I fell asleep under a blanket of pulp?

What if when I woke up a dove flew out of my mouth? What if I
captured the dove and sewed him into the quilt? What if I covered
my children with the quilt? Would they stay warm? Would they
dream of the papery dove? Would they know the dove was their father
flying through their heads?

Three Nests of Cupid

THE ROSE

Cupid coughs and out comes a rose.
The flower's wrath digs a pocket of thorns in Cupid's throat.
He tries to speak but his voice box is filled
With the flower's hot breath which stirs up shiny demons
So Cupid cries diamonds all afternoon.
He goes to the shoreline and walks on ice floes.
He goes to the zoo and walks on ape toes.
There is envy and boredom and the distracting smell of a bakery.
There is his green overcoat, and his thin sunglasses
Hovering over his nose and the traffic.

THE BOAT

Cupid's throat is a moat.
He reaches down deep to pull a soaking poem out of it.
He gurgles to recite it.
The oatmeal moon cackles. The street lights flicker.
A neighbor walking her dog walks faster.
Cupid imagines his children doing somersaults on a boat
Crossing a green ocean to find the land of three-car garages.
His poem trails off into a description

Of a daughter who was never born
And how the robin's nest is whiplashed in the vertigo tree.
How all bodies are eaten pictures,
How the birds drop like leaves of stone.

THE BRAIN

From the ground invisible police cars listen
To Cupid's undocumented brain
Which is sympathetic to the anonymous migrants,
The wounded prisoners, and the misfits milling grain.
These abrasive sounds and feelings confuse the police recording
    device.
It has a migraine and begins to spit out poems:
"I was a star"   "The sky is dirt and skeletons"
"The villain resembles an old bandage"
For a moment the officers are carried off
Into an unlicensed inner playground
But thanks to the blinking lights of the dash cam
They are quickly reinserted among the nipple-less citizens.
Cupid's brain plays another trick.
It imagines rain will make militant islands grow in the air—
The insurrection of mist.

The Iceberg

We were in a dim room where there was
No broom, no fan, not even a vase
So the flowers were shivering when a soundless voice
Touched the two of us and rubbed at our edges
Until we could not tell ourselves apart.
We turned off our phones and closed the windows.
We felt, you'd later say, as though we'd given
Birth to a fierce presence, a bulk that would float
To us like an iceberg, condescending and sinister
Yet somehow something we'd vow to protect,
We'd weep when even small chunks would calve
Into the glassy water. It was all consuming
As though an immense window had opened
Inside me, the one you wanted installed
In the dining room so you could eat a potato
And watch new greenery, the systematic
And intolerable increase over time.

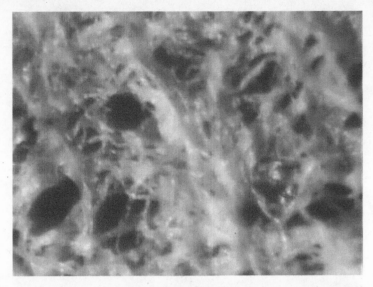

The father of a million particles

In the land of three-car garages

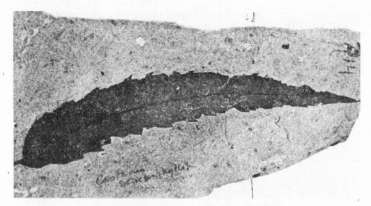

Where the birds drop like leaves of stone

Condescending and sinister

Nests in Air

A new self-sensation is brimming inside me,
You know that electric bug
That crawls up and down the dark window
Writing a gooey cursive.
Is that a suave anthem?

Time and space and pronouns flicker.
If not for you, a night of sleep would remove them.
So what will release me from fraud and error?
That the corn has been harvested?
That the red ants froze to death?

Bugs die, my friend,
But in the case I become edible again,
I grant you this last jackal kiss
Shaved with a decelerating arrow
In the bathroom below the sleeping owl.

The Lakes

When old snow glistens
Little lakes open inside you
Your eyes are lakes
Your mouth is a lake
The rowboat is dumping its cargo

The Unfolding Nest

Wild air, world-mothering air,
Nestling me everywhere…
HOPKINS

After an argument with a friend
I foresee my body losing all its air:

It turns back into a grease stain.
The folded intestines express my personality
And airy consciousness returns to air.

Don't feel bad for the others
I mother inside me—that spoon-fed homunculus
Nestled there in the musty endometrial fold
Or the clustered neural charges clawing
The cortex's bloody warren—

They'll leave this fountain of spit
And follow that seasonal fountain of green
Browning leaves blooming and shedding
Blooming and shedding up and down—

To live outside oneself is happiness.
The mother-presence dwells there forever
Blooming and shedding in ears and nostrils—
    Open ports of sky.

The Nidus

I want to step outside my brain,
Absolve its monologue
And become a small white flower
To shade the robin egg
That fell to the grass
Between the shrubs and chain-link fence.

The doors are locked.
The dark windows reflect the alley's light
And from behind the screen
The father becomes a kind of no-shape,
A reflection in toilette water
Where the warrior brow flattens out
As a bracelet rattles in the bedroom.

That self festers in the cellar,
A mold spawning new colonies
Of devils who have swallowed the scrolls
And digested the passwords.
I try to vomit but what comes out
Is neither human nor invertebrate.
Exoskeletons cannot swim.

Airport Nest

a spell for travelers

In the airport I become a curve
A reedy nest bent around the newborn
Incubating, fingering his plum colored hair
As he sleeps in the green sling
Tied tight behind my shoulder
Though diesel fumes infiltrate the food court
And a watery shadow
Splashes the soapy grime in the public sink
I curve past the gate agent's sparkling eyeliner
I curve along boldface newsstands and pretzels
I hum and count to ten until each number's
A loving arc, and the curve hums the aircraft
Over the runway
And suns and crickets, suns and dew

Bugs die, my friend

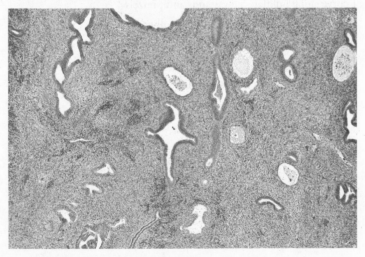

Nestled there in the musty fold

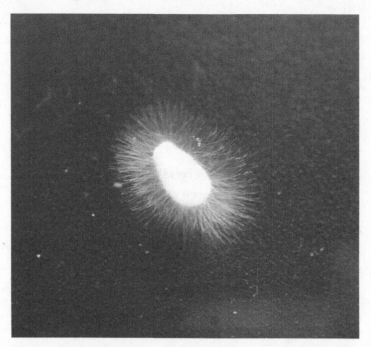

The self in the cellar

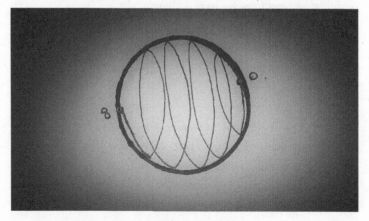

The loving arc

The Cauliflower Nest

for Mom

It's confusing, after eating so much cauliflower
From the serving tray, to find oneself alone
Like this, a cutout on the cutting board long after
The blade has dropped. Whatever is useful
In the cruciferous digestive experience will lodge
Somewhere in the psyche's cluttered nest
So later on, as some foul event runs a flutter,
It might seep into the fissured foundation like
Emergency glue.

              A furry arrow wags toward my
Head but I know it's not a threat. I find
It hard to stay quiet. I say quiet things
Nodding my head though I have nothing to
Say, and in this I am like my mother. My teeth
Are not her teeth, my ears are not her ears.
Her dog's flicking tail has no place in my poem,
Yet it appears,

              arrow-like, its motion stronger
Than any virtue, more virulent than imagery
Or rhythm. It lights up a certain part of the brain,
The way the mere thought of money will ignite
A warm glow around the hypothalamus
But then as it diminishes you wonder whether

You really desired to become better, stronger,
And more circumspect in social and financial
Matters.

    At least my body is a nest, a place
That hums and shivers and burns, a bungalow
To crush with other bodies, other bungalows,
Before becoming the cross-eyed ghoul digging up
Dead pets in the neighbor's backyard graveyard.
A parade of wounds would at least amuse the guests.

The Solar Nest

an overgrown sonnet

The sun massaged my scalp with pencil stubs
And weaved in me the image of a cavern
Where I might store my rock collection. I am
Proudest of the sapphire my friend Daisy rubs
        Between airy fingers.
She loves turquoise blouses and booyah stew,
And takes her Styrofoam coffee to the prairie
To watch with holy hush an inverted flurry
Of bells rising out of anthills. Covered with dew,
        They chime like singers
To descending planes in gray-haired clouds.
They are weaving a nest with a gusty fishing net.
They are teaching children to sing the alphabet.
They are building a factory of musical chairs
        And when they restring their
Dirt-green field, speckled stones float up on a river
Of soil, and in the balding sky kindred spirits shiver.

Atmospheric Peony Incubator

Does it really matter? How she
       Moves the lower lip in a dance?
How her teeth are gemstones
       In a blizzard? How the ochre
Drawing is pinned auspiciously
       Over her bed? How she
Changes the chemical make-up
       Of food with the mutant enzymes
Of fresh saliva? How her foot's arch
       Is the waxing crescent? How
The constellation is her body
       And the clouds of thunder rumble?

Somewhere in the psyche's clutter

Weaving a nest

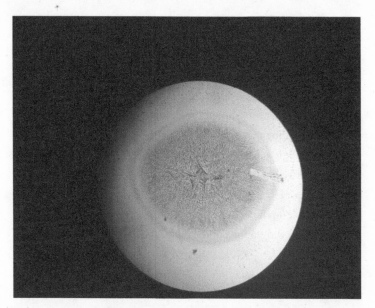

She changes the chemical make-up

The loving arc

Spouse's Refrain

My wife is a needle threading through me,
No, a knot holding me to myself,
And the tighter it gets in here the emptier
I become. I love how she is the tightness and
The emptiness. How she notices me watching
And a sinkhole swallows our house.
It's okay. She is the empress of the dark rubble

Underground where she is like an instinct in my bones
Or an awakening in the endocrine system.
She affixes feathers to the floor with her spit.
She swims with fish at sunrise, sinks a fang into the grotto.
She keeps a stash of chocolate in her purse,
That dark sack where molecules shiver
And spit out small coins. She avoids noodles

But lights up to eat beets straight out of the ground.
Her dirt-red lips burn a campfire in my core.
I can't exactly kiss them but I love how
They singe my lips, chew up the confusion of
Ideology, and spit my teeth into the river
Which I am crossing on smooth wet rocks
And a windy gush splashes us with its bright halo.

Cavity Nesting

a spell to cure allergies

Speck-sized insects creep across the windowsill
While the smell of ferns and new kale and wet dirt
Crawls through the sinus cavities, hollow
Leafy wings inside my face
That lighten the skull so when I walk back inside the house
I won't destroy my temporary consciousness
By sweeping and dusting and tending to dying houseplants.
But some speck-sized organism
Is nesting right there beneath my eyes. What are you,
A tiny screech owl? Something ghostlier? You dwell
Inside my face, some other self of feathers—an allergen
And its muffled midnight trilling sneeze-
Coughs and vomit of pellets, bones, fur.
Next morning the over-sensitive neural transmitter
Contracts my quadriceps. The leg turns into a boner.
Dense pressure slugs the temporal lobe.
The lacrimal sac secretes an ounce of salt water.
I'm no scientist but I'm not really sad. Everything's
A metaphor for everything else. Dead leaves
Droop soilward. I move the plants to the light-filled
Front window and behind
His huffing tears my son wonders: "Why do *I*

Have to go to the grocery store?" "It's just something
We *all have* to *do*. Besides, I love your company.
You help me find the rice cakes."

The Insomniac Nest

a spell for sleep

As I tiptoe through the dark house
My post-meltdown son sleeps peacefully.
His feathers have burned off. The ash infuses
The air with soft spots and medicinal specks.
My bacterial throat opens and my wingy spirit glides
Right through the angel's gasping breathalyzer
And into the pineal gland's melatonin haze.

O Fatherhood, you burn off. You become smoke
Grazing the bank statements, cauterizing
The red ink, thrumming the indolent air.
Don't say indolent. Say cumbersome,
Thumbing the touchscreen, unsatisfied.
Say the news channel ruined your rocking horse,
Its lull, and it lit up your head's homely nucleus
And burnt away that melatonin haze.

Night's swarm of swallows blocks the skylight.
Their shadows too burn off and I am left with
A marriage and a desiccated flowerbed.
Huff huff. The bed's fruit and larvae died off
But one larva ended up alive in the pantry,
Its black screwdriver eyes staring me down

Like *I'm gonna eat your cereal mothafucka*.
My throat opens anyway, and somewhere behind
The eyes resides the hopeful mental greenery
Where the face of the hill peaks in from the haze
With filmic ease to empty that unshuttered heart.

The Larval Son

a vision

Thinking of piñatas
He spontaneously bursts open

He grows butterfly wings and eyes
The grime above the showerhead

He runs his finger over grooves in the banister
In his ribs he feels a hypothetical lion

Could his teeth ravage an entire city?
Could his hands forge a replica in tin?

I'm moving to New Mexico
He says to me over coffee

His eyes flare up
And the fumes smear the chandelier

A clump of leaves drops to my feet—
Who taught him to climb that tree?

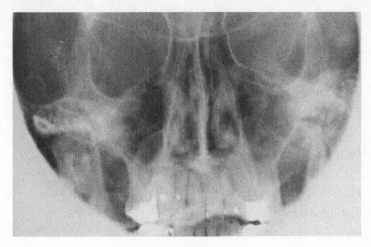

Leafy wings

A constellation, an inroad, a maze

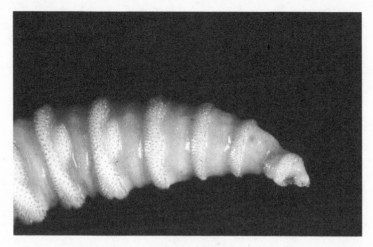

Alive in the pantry

At home within the home

The Sparrow's Nest

a spell for the future, for John Clare

Within my shadow lives a colder shadow,
One devoid of vision or form, a dark fountain
Which reflects my face, and within that face
Is another face: two eyes, a tongue, a constellation
I call "my son," an art form that jibber-jabbers
Into my untuned hearing aid, that inroad
To the greater hive, and within the hive
Is a maze of chambers housing more sons
And daughters and mahogany bureaus
And pleated accordion drapes. Behind the drapes
Are my daughters' daughters who carry earthworms
From the garden and sing and breathe and belch.
Soon they'll wear lipstick and give birth
Maybe to twins, and I'll wash my hands
Before holding the babies, and beneath the soap dish
Is the shadow soap dish, the oil, the grime,
The slippery outline that haunts the soap
And the twisty timeline ghost-riding through me,
And inside the slippery outline I exhaust my homilies
At home within the home within the shady leaves.

Nests in Air

Another bird comes to my window.
Like me, it needs to be released
From the electromagnetic hell
It carries in its little head.
Like me, it lost its warble, maybe beneath
The moldy potatoes stacked in the silo.
Maybe in the dead squirrel's stomach.
Maybe in the lizard's glass box
Which smells of wood chips and animal
Which is why no one visits the house.

Is the bird looking for the wall of butterflies?
Or the wall of sound that houses the queen
Whose eyes make our stomachs warble?
She loves vermouth and marbles.
She loves to mouth her ice water
And builds pendant nests with mud and reeds
And candy wrappers that the wind
Blew into the yard.
When she winks, the yard fills up with snow.
When she sighs, the sky infiltrates the shed.
Sometimes her sentences stop in the middle,
Waxing half moons that slam into reverse.

She wants the moonlight to go back
To the shade it was before the fern died.
She knows the reedy bird must shiver
But may no longer sing, trying to ignore the buzzing sky
Which is blue though not the jewel the mind makes
As it envisions the child's face reflected on the steel silo.
The face in the window. The face in the tree.
The face in the cupboard with sugar, vanilla, and tea.

Lear's Nest

If the smell of burning toast were to waft into my dream, how would I respond? Would I fear that our old house was burning down? Would I envision a magic fire hose covering the embers in a blanket of foam?

If the foam hardened into a surface of ice, would my children play a game of hockey on it? Would they bash each other's heads in with their sticks? Would they knock out my eyes with the puck?

Would they stuff my eye sockets with the ice chips and shroud me in a new darkness, a new vision? Would they dress me in rags and lead me off the rink, out of the house, into the street where the ambulance and fire trucks have crashed into each other because they were so eager to respond to the emergency?

Which child would lead me by the hand? Would she feed me hot soup, buttered toast, and a love richer than the tongue? Would she be my new favorite, a songbird, burnt orange, on acorns, dropped, dropped straight from the catalpa?

Homer Simpson at Key West

Egg-eyed Homer Simpson gestures toward the sea.
Each hand lacks one finger, for the artist's psychic wounds
Have manifested themselves in mimetic truncations.
Homer thinks the fluttering in his stomach is one
Of hunger's many waves, but it is merely the off-screen artist's urge
To reshape the emblazoned zone, that tilting nest
Wherein sound and image embellish the offspring,
Their empty sleeves and inhuman cries in acutely colored gullies.
And although flowers grow all around Springfield,
The Nuclear Plant dumps tons of sludge in the dark gray river
Where the mutated fish blow vast thought bubbles
Straight into the filthy water supply pipes. That delicate death-rattler
Mr. Burns has appropriated many sectors of the city's wild space
And even amid the rare botany, Homer's stomach is legendary.
He once ate 64 slices of American cheese during a sleepless night.
But today the crooked frigatebird he spots on the horizon
Zigzags like a caretaker's maze, I mean the parent's conflicted feelings
Of boredom and responsibility, which even Homer feels,
So when you sing to your baby you are merely shuffling the gasping
    wind
And the sea and a bird's elongated warbles which we swore we heard
At precisely the same time each morning a moment before the dawn.
Now Homer hears nothing, not the grinding water, not the heaving
    sky.

His ear-holes are small, whale-like, and he fears his sleep's wavy
    information.
He drinks another Duff, this one pouring straight into his mouth
In a rapid column from at least six inches over his head
As if some sprite had lifted the can and tilted it at the perfect angle
But of course it is his son, Bart, whose yellow body is the spirit of
    impish
World-making that infuriates Homer—*his* wandering from hour to
    hour
In the summer without end means that even the theatrical distances
Of each digesting hamburger might rekindle Marge's magic blue hair,
Might make the speech accutest song, might enchant the night,
That thread between the indifferent overweight father and his
    children
Whose keen laughter deepens the sea's color and demarcates
The irony of the desire to steal a fishing boat and set out
To return with fish that will become the coins that will buy the family
    bread.

The Mole's Nest, or The Ear's Revenge

In the opera called "The Mole's Nest"
An ear-shaped stranger finds himself lost
In a dark forest but soon arrives at a kingdom
Embroiled in a long civil war. The Ear's recitativo
Describes a small knife that shears away
The suburban lawns. This vision haunts the soprano
Who recognizes the Ear's messianic vision.
She tries to hide it from her father, the deluded king,
But her fiancé, the self-proclaimed Prince Avian,
Gives away the Ear's hideout
In the copse of hornlike pines.
In the third act, her father the deluded king
Stuffs the Ear with several pounds of wet
Compressed cotton balls. He will make the Ear his slave—
Use it as a nest to incubate a new strain
Of microbial spies that will help thwart
The kingdom's pesky insurgents. Alone in its glass cage
The Ear sings a long lament on being trapped
In a conflict to which it is indifferent.
And although it is only a representation of an ear,
A man-sized piece of whirling plaster,
The audience feels uneasy, as though
A crumb or feather were stuck in their throats.
They shift in their seats. They massage their Adam's apples

And quietly gag. The rhythmic choking
Unravels an uneasy skybound ecstasy,
A collective consciousness that unfolds like a blue light
Pushing, prying, peeling at the offstage limits
Until, with a sudden crash, the soprano smashes a teacup
Against her father's head. She has inherited
A nervous tic from her tribe's history of genocidal rampage.
"No," she sings in the final aria's refrain, "I don't want to dream.
I want to watch the mole spit poison on the worms
Before their stiff bodies drop into his moistened nest."

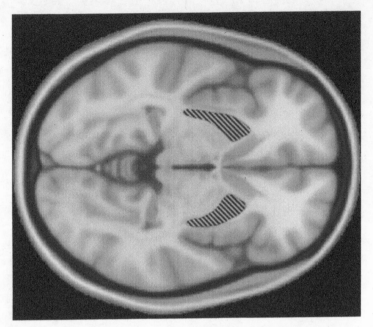

The electromagnetic hell

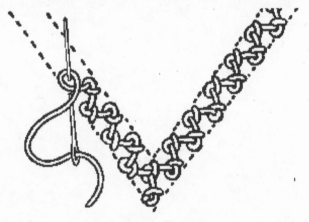

The caretaker's maze

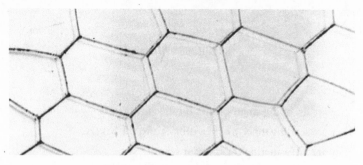

Would my children play hockey on it?

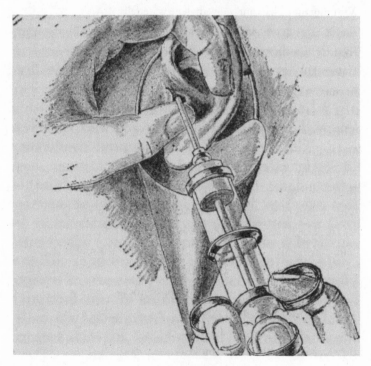

The nest of microbial spies

The Barbed Wire Nest

They are dropping smart bombs on the glue factory.
They are sending saber-toothed drones into the bakery.
They are inseminating the migrant seamstress
And repopulating the mountain states
With mutant jackals and polyethylene waterfalls.
They are selling our skin cells to the cosmetic surgeons.
They are dismembering nude mannequins
And stacking the spikey limbs in the courtyard
So you can climb the pile and peek over the barbed wire
For a glimpse at the newly upholstered boardroom
Where they are declawing the help staff
And drafting the bill to outlaw the law.
They plan to kick us with steel-tipped boots
Then they'll stuff us with arsenic and gag us
With clumps of hot tar. They'll assassinate the cartoonists
And fuck each other on hardbacks in the library
Before incinerating the archives with antique flamethrowers.
They'll arm the snowmen with Uzis
And bury the bookkeeper under the mossy rocks
In the backyard with the beekeeper
And the beehive's desiccated hull.
They'll take a breath, have a smoke,
And paint our eyelids shut with organic honey—
So while I still have a face inside my face

I try to look at them with the most objective eye.
And hold the breath inside my breath
Until a flood of light washes over my body
And when the body has been consumed
The server brings back my debit card
And the thin slip of paper and the almost inkless pen
And when I turn to sign the paper
The strap of my dress falls over my shoulder.
The pendant nest suspends the breeze.
The sunflower swivels its shadow.

The Resurrection Nest

When the windshield-splattered gnats are reborn
They'll want to dismantle our automobiles
And tear up the roads and parking lots.
They'll trip up the pedestrians and tip over the strollers.
They won't even forgive the cyclists.
They'll want to fly in our ears
And stitch together great clumps of wax.
If you listen, you can hear them plotting
Beneath the radio silence. If you listen
You can feel their looping flight patterns
Knotting the clouds to our pockets
So I sit in a dark room   my eyes closed
And I plead with the creature to go back inside
And I try to remember a song about a shadow
That swallowed the suburbs.
Even in the self-referential loop
The simplest connotations go haywire.
The woven grass tightens its hold.

No matter how hard you look
You won't spot the gnats coming.
Instead in the distance you may see a straw bonnet
Borne aloft in the wind, and someone else's bayonet
Stabbing through the curtains, while

Someone's snow blower spews mud on the sidewalks
And the superhighways sprout skeletons
So without thinking someone unscrews the doorjamb
And someone pulls out a roll of bandages
And someone awkwardly mentions the president
Shouldn't he be making a speech?
Shouldn't he explain our next exit strategy?
Should we build a museum and hide in the diorama?
So someone paints his face on the brick wall.
Under the presidential gaze
A father hands his briefcase to his baby.
The hummingbirds suck down the airwaves.
The impossible animal emerges.
The impossible animal emerges, but no poem
Will clean the cages or perfume their odors.

A Father's Work Is Never Done

Father was tired of gender so he entered a trance and conceived the
 Holy Ghost,
A neuter spirit that would ride alongside him as he drove his dark red
 Saturn up the mountain of the future.
And he drove up the mountain of the future and deforested most of it
 and built luxury condos on the southwest slopes
And he relocated the wolves, which were dear as children to him, in
 zoos so large the zookeepers were still mapping out the boundaries.
Then the Holy Ghost got lost in a pack of storm clouds, which was
 the plan from the beginning for even in the beginning
Father's plans were complex and ineffable.
Father's plans were beautiful as scrambled eggs.
Father's plans were difficult to digest, and the more we asked about
 them the more we felt butter churning in our stomachs.
And he devised this plan: in the future English will be a moustache
 that slowly leaks hot oil into the mouth.
And he devised this plan: we'll stand on our heads and let the ocean
 wash over us.
The ocean will be a tub of mint tea.
The ocean will make the sound of a tuba and be filled with manatees.
He devised another plan and took a nap.
His nap was a long summer day and in his dream he conceived new
 names for his children

And he awoke with a start and let out a yelp when they began
 clipping his whiskers.
They clubbed each other with magic police wands and smeared blood
 on his Saturn's windshield.
It was a homecoming party and they needed to build a nest.
They needed to crawl back into that monster's mouth.

Suspend the breeze

Father's plans

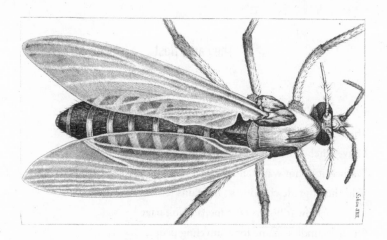

Dismantle the automobiles

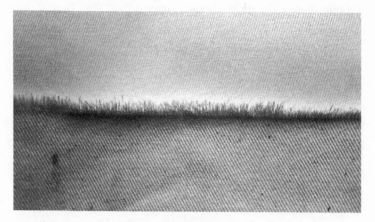

Hover over me

The Paper Nest

1.

The white flag unfurls below pearly flat clouds.
I have stitched its holes with thin synthetic fibers,
Washed it in hot water and sprayed it down
With hotel-grade chlorine so no stains remain.

      Now it hovers over me, a blank page
Or the soundless name for a sniveling people
Of bird-like fear, the unwritten name for a people
Of thin talons and weak bones and crumpled
Digestive tracts. It is the flapping name

      For a people of psychotic glowing gadgets
People of daggers. Live streaming people. TV people
They flash lightningwhite teeth, and in their dopey eyes
You can read a history of seasalt, of seahags
Burning crosses and large snouted mammals.

      When I think about their people hair
I want to drink green liquor, and when I think
About their people eyes I want to split a fruit fly in half
Its genetic sequence births a poem so long and boring that

      When I read it I feel like a people
Is shoveling sand into my open skull—why is my skull open?
Is it a holiday? Should I be eating ham?
I don't know, I drink that green people drink
And this rattling person called "I" defaces all the people-paper.

Is this person just my head's
Overcaffeinated meta-commentator, an oily person-voice
That describes drinking as a metaphor for reading
And reading as a metaphor for a people's territorial expansion?
It sounds congested. Here, have a Benadryl, depopulate yourself.
Leave your phosphorescent coin wrapped in Kleenex on the bar
          And the zinc glows.

2.

          But the faces
All their orange and blue eyes pop out of the overhanging
Television. They say: Here, drink this bottle of bleach
          And white out your inner life.
Here, massage this penguin oil into your person scalp
It will help your skull maintain its seedy melon shape
And soothe the hoarse meta-commentator.
          Swallow this eco-friendly loaf of bread.
Dial this rotary phone and confess—confess
Everything confess all your viper thoughts
To the notsofriendly operator: this call may be monitored
And/or recorded for quality and training purposes.
          So don't hold back, tell how you're not
A person, you're a voice on paper, and you're afraid
To turn the page because it's hiding a revolver.
Cock it and aim at the person-shaped cloud
          Slouching in your paper mirror.
Cock it and flog yourself. Interrogate your paper cat.

Put your family on notice. They are paper people
And paper burns. Cock it and bulldoze
      Your paper people family farm.
Dump your radishes in the people river.
Tie writhing knots with the snakes in the hayloft.
Cock your old papery revolver. Cock it and let
Its clicking be an endless winter on the filthy, flat, bare
      Bulldozed family farm.

High-Definition Nest

The post-apocalyptic father attaches another rooftop
To the farmhouse. The soup's on, and it's hot.
The crows eye it from the crooked birch.
Envisioning a fire, the post-identity family stitches their buttons to
     their noses.
It's a tribal thing. Without history. As if an unlicensed mirror
Were running the Office of Light Projection
But no one walks through the blood stained territories
Where the post-chemical thugs siphon great subsidies
For longer mandated testing. And the post-monetary bankers
Keep erasing the contents of their thought bubbles.
They know the rules:
                         There can be no evidence,
No record of an internal monologue or other outmoded humanist
     tropes.
They know the biggest swindle is the imagination,
An excruciating and invisible nest
That, like a minute infection, opens doorways
And archways and walkways into the sun—

                                        Ghoulish sun

Breeding maggots on post-burial corpses—
Ghoulish sun showing an animated spider that walks across the water,

While my family coughs out their neon-flavored soup
In the post-clinical emergency room.
Would you let me hiccup in that polyester pillow?
Can I spit the imagination into this box of rubber gloves?
Can I borrow this scalpel to carve away my makeup?
Mysterious bells ring in the post-musical ears—
They're covered in lichen, they're blooming green ether.
Back in the kitchen I'll chisel the scallions—they wither so quickly.
They're not cut out for the twenty-four second news cycle.
I'll fold them in quarters and drop them in the soup.

The Wasp Nest

When I was young, I got a buzz off buying things.
In our garage beneath their nest I'd find
Broken or brittle wasp bodies and exchange
Them with the shadows for dead souls, plumes of smoke
Wordlessly discharged straight into my sweatshirt
Pockets. Revolutionary politics

Emerged after the removal of the nest, a politics
Of wavy pulses, a rhythm felt beneath all things
And people, dead insects, buildings, fabrics, sweatshirts,
Clumps of hair, whatever else you find
In front of your face or covered in the smoke
Of habits, the eating, sleeping, and hurried exchange

Of goods and services. But who can exchange
The child for the man when callous politics
Slams us aggressively through the streets, into smoke
And pesticides? It's a slick steppingstone that quickens things
Until life's not what we'd thought we'd find.
There must be more than the lint the sweatshirt

Lodged in my belly button. Wearing that sweatshirt
My belly always sweats but the sixty-day exchange
Period has already passed. That flea market find

Was one of many disappointments to blame on politics,
How it stings us with dazzling speeches so all things
Glint like black hair. How it blows thick smoke

From the growing mountain of ash, smoke
From the mound of dead wasps and burning sweatshirts.
Smoke from the irretrievable honey and sleep—things
In which I believe—things which have no exchange
Value. Zilch. A leaf comes apart in my hand. O Politics
Thou art sick. The Invisible Worm will find

Your eggs in their brooding cells, suck them empty, and find
You in the picnic shelter where the grill smoke
Conditions the wood rafters. Rub your fingers, Politics,
Over these poems—warm them in old sweatshirts
And take from the pocket last year's papery fibers to exchange
For cracked glass, used stingers, and other broken things.

You'll buzz so loud when you find among these things
A new queen hibernating in smoky ice. Don't shiver. Exchange
Her body of hazy politics for a breathable sweatshirt.

Nests in Air

When I draw a bath for my six-year-old
He is copying in cursive his story
About the wild man who upon finally shaving
His massive beard saw how sloppy
His mouth had become, a deranged half-moon
Hanging slightly to the left side
Of his sun-red face. Like all medieval folk,
The man aspired to a seat at the Round Table,
But this was no way for a good knight
To appear. An airborne mother wrote him
A coded message in the clouds but only
The key hidden in his dead father's jerkin
Would unlock its meaning: six simple steps
To the everyday work of emotional recovery
Where masculine neurons ignite an emblazoned
Zone of energetic fruit. The man put away
His sword and digested the seeds.
Night limped forward...

                        At that point my son's
Handwriting became a gnarled mass of lines—
A scribbled heap of twine—a nest of helpless
Body rhythms that birthed, as a new fragrant

Dimension, an indefinitely-shaped lake lapping
Against steep granite bluffs while overhead
Fly fire-red day birds in night-swirling swoops
And the looming despots turn to cloud.

Nests in Air

This afternoon I'm not thinking
    about politics
I'm removing an overgrown shrub
    from the front yard
When my son interrupts waving
    a flashlight from
Eye to eye and scares the fuck
    out of me my flesh
Freezes a breeze blows the chalk
    off the walkway
And unhinges the chain links
    of the old fence
When the sky's metallic sphere
    rolls straight back
The breeze weaves us a new
    baby blue sky
What does it want? How has it
    soundlessly unzipped
Its militant architecture?
It is vigorous pecking
    or a careful net
Repairing the orchestra of sparrows

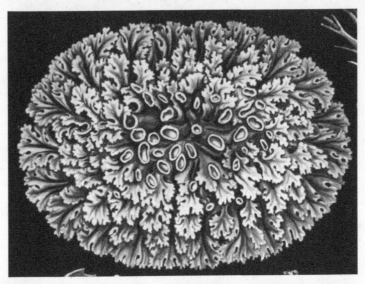

In the post-musical ears

An exchange

A rhythm beneath all things

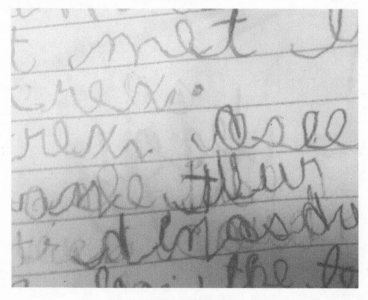

A new fragrant dimension

ACKNOWLEDGEMENTS

Some of these poems originally appeared in *Hyperallergic*, *Bat City Review*, the *Harvard Review Online*, the Academy of American Poets' *Poem a Day Series*, *Matter Monthly*, *Sprung Formal*, *Golden Shovel Anthology*, *Kettle Blue Review*, *Conduit*, the *New Orleans Review*, *H_ng-m_n*, *Alaska Quarterly Review*, *Muse/A*, *Typo*, and *Fence*. Thank you to the editors!

Big thanks to all who have sustained me, aiding and abetting the writing of this book: Nikki Flores, Teddy Hoks, James Shea, Chris and Kasey Hund, Jason and Kelly Zech, Joe Bienvenu, Joel Craig, Chad Chmielowicz, Katie Wilson, Jared Stanley, Maung Day, Dean Young, Rachel Galvin, Joe Pan, Matthew Corey, John Wilkinson, Jorge Sanchez, Elizabeth Wetmore, Jennifer Karmin, Daniel Borzutzky, Sara Wainscott, Anthony Madrid, Matt Hart, Hai-Dang Phan, Miha Maurič, Ivan Antić, and my parents (all six of you!).

Thank you, too, Black Ocean's crew, especially Janaka Stucky and Carrie Olivia Adams, for their generosity, guidance, and support.

* * *

Several poems borrow scraps from and/or are dialogue with work by Guillaume Apollinaire, John Ashbery, Georges Bataille, Elizabeth

Bishop, William Blake, Gwendolyn Brooks, John Clare, Samuel Taylor Coleridge, Gilles Deleuze, T. S. Eliot, Félix Guattari, Gerard Manley Hopkins, John Keats, Bernadette Mayer, Alice Notley, Arthur Rimbaud, Wallace Stevens, William Wordsworth, John Yau, & probably others I'm forgetting.

IMAGE CREDITS

Each set of four images may be considered a nest, a visual space that has been "tagged" with lines (often modified) from the preceding poems. All of the images are in the public domain and were found on Wikimedia Commons by searching keywords from the poems. Thank you to the various photographers and artists. Here are the original descriptions as uploaded to Wikimedia:

Blocking out the moonlight. Honey bee swarm, by Temtem. https://commons.wikimedia.org/wiki/File:Beeswarm1.jpg

The polyethylene compounds plug up my nose. Polyethylene balls, by Lluis tgn. https://commons.wikimedia.org/wiki/File:Polyethylene_balls1.jpg

Something shrill in the eye sings out. Scanning electron microscope image of an eye on a fruit fly, by Louisa Howard. https://commons.wikimedia.org/wiki/File:Drosophilidae_compound_eye.jpg

I peck-peck-peck at the mush-mush-mush. A box of recyclable mixed paper pulp at the Eco Experience building at the Minnesota State Fair on August 29, 2018, by Tony Webster. https://commons.wikimedia.org/wiki/File:Recycled_Mixed_Paper_Pulp,_Post-Consumer_Recyclable_Waste_(42555846610).jpg

A powerful glow. Sunflower head (Helianthus annuus) Felsőtold,

Hungary, by Takkk. https://commons.wikimedia.org/wiki/
File:Sunflower_head_(Helianthus_annuus)_Hungary_Felsotold.jpg

When I crinkle the newspaper. Simulated napalm explosion, official
USMC photo by LCpl Andrew Pendracki. https://commons.
wikimedia.org/wiki/File:Simulated_Napalm_Airstrike.jpg

Dust rises toward my rolled cuffs. Comets Kick up Dust in Helix
Nebula, by NASA/JPL-Caltech/Univ. of Ariz. https://commons.
wikimedia.org/wiki/File:Comets_Kick_up_Dust_in_Helix_
Nebula_(PIA09178).jpg

Beams warp around the pines. Fireworks in Abstract—Abstract photo
experiments taken at the 2015 Vancouver Celebration of Light
fireworks, by inabstracting. https://commons.wikimedia.org/wiki/
File:Beam_(24695932214).jpg

The father of a million particles. 80X Microscopic image of pulp in
tissue paper, by Ciphers. https://commons.wikimedia.org/wiki/
File:Tissue_pulp_80X.JPG

The land of three-car garages. Aerial view of suburban Levittown,
Pennsylvania.https://commons.wikimedia.org/wiki/
File:LevittownPA.jpg

Where the birds drop like leaves of stone. Fossil chestnut leaf castanea
dolichophylla, from *Popular Science Monthly Volume 73, 1908.*
https://commons.wikimedia.org/wiki/File:PSM_V73_D127_
Fossil_chestnut_leaf_castanea_dolichophylla.png

Condescending and sinister. Glaçot avec sa partie submergée clairement
visible (Iceberg with submerged portion clearly visible), by
Individuo. https://commons.wikimedia.org/wiki/File:Iceberg_
with_submerged_portion_clearly_visible.jpg

Bugs die, my friend! Red ants in Lambir Hills NP, Sarawak, Malaysia, by Bernard Dupont.https://commons.wikimedia.org/wiki/ File:Red_Ants_(8440494017).jpg

Nestled there in the musty fold. Nucleated red blood cells—endometrial polyp, by Nephron.https://commons.wikimedia.org/wiki/ File:Nucleated_red_blood_cells_-_endometrial_polyp_-_low_ mag.jpg

The self in the cellar. Water mold Mizukabi colony. https://commons. wikimedia.org/wiki/File:Water_mold_Mizukabi_colony.jpg

The loving arc. "Here Vay 4 is spiral drawn inside a circle.where one point indicates 'o' and another point is'∞.' Anything present in our universe has end. which means like a loop or circle(having starting point suppose 'o' point to ending point is '∞' like in vay 4 image). Every solution,matter, elements and anything present on this universe certain medium which has its own boundaries like closed. If we are at closed boundary there is no infinity '∞' and it has some value. Like if we take 'o' as starting point and ending or infinity point(∞) as 1..Then we get correct path from zero to infinity by assuming 'o' to '1.'Here on vay 4 image has circle is o to ∞. So we no need to go through line of circle.we can go through spiral,which is shortest way to travel 'o' to '∞.' What i mean is our living timeline is also a closed boundary.If we find shortcut path like rectangular,square,straight line and spiral inside a closed boundary or a loop.Then we can cross timeline as our wish like time travel.we can create loop holes which will make our universe as small. for example: If ant is thinking like scientist it says that earth is infinite.Similarly here humans in this universe.Here spiral is the best way to cross any point in the universe to another point. Because spiral has many connection to closed boundary.so we can cross any points easily…," by Vishva teja. https://commons. wikimedia.org/wiki/File:Vay_4.jpg

Somewhere in the psyche's clutter. Fraktaler Blumenkohl, by Micha L. Rieser. https://commons.wikimedia.org/wiki/File:Blumenkohl_ fraktal.jpg

Weaving a nest. Fishing net in Karystos, Euboea, Greece, by Jebulon. https://commons.wikimedia.org/wiki/File:Fishing_net_Karystos_ Euboea_Greece.jpg

She changes the chemical make-up. Microcristalling of saliva of small saliva glands, by IlyaFrolovo9. https://commons.wikimedia.org/ wiki/File:%D0%9C%D0%B8%D0%BA%D1%80%D0%BE%D0 %BA%D1%80%D0%B8%D1%81%D1%82%D0%B0%D0%BB% D0%BB%D0%B8%D0%B7%D0%B0%D1%86%D0%B8%D1% 8F_%D1%81%D0%BB%D1%8E%D0%BD%D1%8B_%D0%B- C%D0%B0%D0%BB%D1%8B%D1%85_%D1%81%D0%BB%D1 %8E%D0%BD%D0%BD%D1%8B%D1%85_%D0%B6%D0%B5 %D0%BB%D1%91%D0%B7.jpg

I become empty. Sackknop, by Sebbe. https://commons.wikimedia. org/wiki/File:Sackknop.jpg

Leafy wings. Roentgenology of the Maxillary Sinuses … Shows both of the maxillary sinuses, as well as the ethmoidal and frontal sinuses in normal condition. From *Oral Roentgenology : a Roentgen study of the anatomy and pathology of the oral cavity*, Boston, Mass. : Ritter & Company, 1917, by Kurt H. Thoma. https://commons. wikimedia.org/wiki/File:Oral_Roentgenology_-_a_Roentgen_

study_of_the_anatomy_and_pathology_of_the_oral_cavity_
(1917)_(14754620821).jpg

Alive in the pantry. Screw Worm Fly Larvae Through Electron
Microscope, by Entomology, CSIRO https://commons.wikimedia.
org/wiki/File:CSIRO_ScienceImage_115_The_Tip_of_a_Screw_
Worm_Fly_Larvae.jpg

A constellation, an inroad, a maze. Abhandlungen aus dem
Gebiete der Naturwissenschaften, from Naturwissenschaftlicher
Verein, Hamburg, 1846. https://commons.wikimedia.org/wiki/
File:Abhandlungen_aus_dem_Gebiete_der_Naturwissenschaften_
(1856)_(16716322731).jpg

At home within the home. Song Sparrow nest, by Tony Alter. https://
commons.wikimedia.org/wiki/File:Song_Sparrow_nest_with_eggs.
jpg

The electromagnetic hell. Putamen, by Woutergroen. https://
commons.wikimedia.org/wiki/File:Putamen.jpg

Would my children play hockey on it? 2-dimensional foam (bubbles
lie in one layer; colors inverted), by Klaus-Dieter Keller. https://
commons.wikimedia.org/wiki/File:2-dimensional_foam_(colors_
inverted).jpg

The caretaker's maze. Turk's head knot, from *Samplers and Stitches*,
a handbook of the embroiderer's art by Mrs Archibald Christie,
London 1920. https://commons.wikimedia.org/wiki/File:Zig-
zag_coral_stitch.gif

The nest of microbial spies. from *An American text-book of the diseases
of children*, Philadelphia, W.B. Saunders, 1895, by Louis Starr and
Thompson Seiser Westcott. https://commons.wikimedia.org/

wiki/File:An_American_text-book_of_the_diseases_of_children_
(1895)_(14595753590).jpg

Suspend the breeze. Pendant nest of the Baltimore Oriole, from *Bird
homes : the nests, eggs and breeding habits of the land birds breeding
in the eastern United States*, New York : Doubleday, Page, 1902, by
Arthur Radclyffe Dugmore. https://commons.wikimedia.org/wiki/
File:Bird_homes_-_the_nests,_eggs_and_breeding_habits_of_the_
land_birds_breeding_in_the_eastern_United_States;_with_hints_
on_the_rearing_and_photographing_of_young_birds_(1902)_
(14568874537).jpg

Dismantle the automobiles. "The great Belly'ed Gnat or female Gnat".
An illustration of a Gnat thought to have been drawn by Sir
Christopher Wren, from *MICROGRAPHIA or some physiological
descriptions of minute bodies made by magnifying glasses with
observations and inquiries thereupon*, by Robert Hooke, 1665.
https://commons.wikimedia.org/wiki/File:Hooke-gnat.jpg

Father's plans. Just some ol eggs in the oven, by RHBlair. https://
commons.wikimedia.org/wiki/File:Eggs_in_the_Oven.JPG

Hover over me. Cotton bleaching before and after, by Aboalbiss.
https://commons.wikimedia.org/wiki/File:Cotton_bleaching_
befor_and_after.jpg

In the post-musical ears. Kunstformen der Natur (1904), plate 83:
Lichenes. https://commons.wikimedia.org/wiki/File:Haeckel_
Lichenes.jpg

A rhythm beneath all things. Paper wasp nest at night, built on a shed's
overhang, photographed with a flash, by Angrylambie. https://
commons.wikimedia.org/wiki/File:Paper_wasp_nest.jpg

An exchange. Broken Glass, by Rodrigo Paredes. https://commons. wikimedia.org/wiki/File:Broken_Glass_(18434524128).jpg

A new fragrant dimension. Child's handwriting. Photograph by the author.